BOOKS BY J.R. SOLONCHE

POEMS

Old
Then Morning
Reading Takuboku Ishikawa
God
The Architect's House
The Eglantine
Leda
Alone
The Book of a Small Fisherman
The Dreams of the Gods
Around Here
The Lost Notebook of Zhao Li
The Five Notebooks of Zhao Li
Life-Size
Coming To
Selected Poems 2002 – 2021
Years Later
The Dust
A Guide of the Perplexed
The Moon Is the Capital of the World
For All I Know
The Time of Your Life
Enjoy Yourself
Piano Music
The Porch Poems
The Jewish Dancing Master
In a Public Place
If You Should See Me Walking on the Road
To Say the Least
True Enough
In Short Order
Tomorrow, Today, and Yesterday
Invisible
Won't Be Long
I, Emily Dickinson & Other Found Poems
Heart's Content
The Black Birch
Beautiful Day
Peach Girl: Poems for a Chinese Daughter (with Joan I. Siegel)

CRITICISM

An Aesthetic Toward Notes: On Poets & Poetry

NIGHT VISIT

J. R. SOLONCHE

DOS MADRES
2024

DOS MADRES PRESS INC.
P.O. Box 294, Loveland, Ohio 45140
www.dosmadres.com   editor@dosmadres.com

Dos Madres is dedicated to the belief that the small press is essential to the vitality of contemporary literature as a carrier of the new voice, as well as the older, sometimes forgotten voices of the past. And in an ever more virtual world, to the creation of fine books pleasing to the eye and hand.

Dos Madres is named in honor of Vera Murphy and Libbie Hughes, the "Dos Madres" whose contributions have made this press possible.

Dos Madres Press, Inc. is an Ohio Not For Profit Corporation and a 501 (c) (3) qualified public charity. Contributions are tax deductible.

Executive Editor: Robert J. Murphy

Illustration & Book Design: Elizabeth H. Murphy
www.illusionstudios.net

Typeset in Adobe Garamond Pro & Lithos
ISBN 978-1-962847-17-9
Library of Congress Control Number: 2024950618

First Edition
Copyright 2024 J. R. Solonche
All rights reserved. No part of this book may be reproduced or transmitted in any form or by any means graphic, electronic or mechanical, including photocopying, recording, taping or by any information storage or retrieval system, without the permission in writing from the publisher.
Published by Dos Madres Press, Inc.

Table of Contents

Part I

Night Visit 1
I Thought of God 2
The Secret 3
The Civil War 4
Chivalry 5
A Memory 6
If I Could Make Up 7
Q & A 8
On My Birthday 9
The Families 10
A Glass Bottle Almost Like a Woman 11
Dementia 12
The Radio 13
My Student 14
Shit 15
How to Fold 16
Deaf Child Area 17
Minds 18
Roses 19
Whiskey 20
Time 21
Moons 22
All the Rest 23
Late July Pastoral 24
Six Crows and Their Shadows 25

Dementia 26
Unburdened 27
What's in a Name 28
Coward 29
Reading 30
St. Anne 31
Thistles 32
In the Store 33
Physical Therapy 34
Orthodox Paradox 35
Short August Pastoral 36
Margie 37

PART II

I, Too, Have Nowhere 41
I, Too, Have Been Married 42
I, Too, Learn from the Lake 43
The Big Hornets 44
Sympathy 45
Squatters in the Planter 46
My Plumber Is a Sculptor 47
August Lament 48
Nina Simone 49
Balcony 50
Beyond the Pale 51
Momentous 52
Debate 53
No Contest 54

Dementia	55
In the Liquor Store	56
The Journey	57
Soul	58
The Face	59
Like You, Alfred	60
Unlike You, Alfred	61
A Hawk with a Broken Wing Is a Hawk Broken	62
Columbus	63
False Messiah	65
A Photograph of William Carlos Williams	66
Rhinoceros Head	67
The Best Names in Poetry	68
When the Buddha Was 80 Years Old	72
A Green Glass Bottle	73
Angina	74
Where	76
About the Author	79

PART I

NIGHT VISIT

There is supposed to be a city,
a city that comes out only at night,
not in dreams but in actuality
like a miracle, like the moon, like the stars,
but the city I see when I step outside
on a summer night is the city of the crickets.
Ah, is it not a pity that we are not in Andalucia?

I THOUGHT OF GOD

I thought of god.
I thought of god thinking.
He looked like Rodin's *The Thinker* with a long white beard.
He was tired of resting.
He was bored.
He was thinking of creating something new and spectacular.
"I think a black hole would be something new and spectacular,"
    he thought.
"It should be quite simple," he thought.
"I'll just poke my forefinger into space.
Then I'll twirl it around until a hole opens up," he thought.
So he chuckled and created a black hole.
It was so simple and so much fun, he created millions of them.
He put a black hole in the center of every galaxy.
"Now I'll sit back, relax, and enjoy the action," he thought.
And he sat back and relaxed – as much as a throne allows.
And he enjoyed the action – as much as a Jewish god can
    enjoy anything.

THE SECRET

I marvel at them,
the petunias, the purple,
the white, the variegated,
upright, high-headed again in the sun
now out after downpours of days on end.
As usual, the secret is in the roots.

THE CIVIL WAR

A Quaker Union
officer wrote to his
mother not to worry
because he didn't
kill anyone himself
but only ordered his
men to.

CHIVALRY

A hummingbird sits
on the hook that holds
the feeder, waiting for
the butterfly to leave.

A MEMORY

When I was six, I had my
tonsils out. The doctor told
me to count backward from
a hundred. I don't know why.
I was six. I couldn't count even
forward. It didn't matter, though.
The ether put me out fast. When
I woke up, a nurse brought me
an ice cream cup, half chocolate,
half vanilla, and a wooden spoon.
I miss that ice cream. It was the best
I've ever had. I miss that wooden
spoon. It was the best I've ever had
with ice cream. Most of all, I miss
that nurse, and even though the
light in the recovery room was
dim, and I couldn't see her face
very well, she was the most
beautiful woman I've ever seen,
that nurse who gave me that ice
cream with that wooden spoon
when I was six.

IF I COULD MAKE UP

If I could make up a mythological creature,
she would be a mermaid with wings or an angel
with a fish tail, for then she could be at home
everywhere save dry land, and only the cleverest
and the bravest of mortal men could ever catch her
and hold her and look into her eyes and lie with her.

Q & A

"What do women want?"
asked Freud.

"What does poetry want?"
I ask.

"The same,"
answers Freud.

"The same,"
I answer.

ON MY BIRTHDAY

It was 1946.
It was the 16th of July.
It was 4:22 in the afternoon.
It was when I was born.
It changed my life.

THE FAMILIES

They are still around,
the Crists, the Bulls,
the Ramsdels, the Howells,
their names on the roads
so far from where they fell.

A GLASS BOTTLE ALMOST LIKE A WOMAN

A Rubens woman,
not a modern woman,
heavy at the top,
and though pinched
below the bosom,
still enough heft at the waist
where the hand securely
holds and turns right and
turns left.

DEMENTIA

On her face, no, not
on, her face itself is pure
laugh, but laughterless,
larger than I've ever
seen, and longer. Is it
a smile then since it is
soundless and longer
than any sensible laugh
should last? Or for that
matter, any smile?

THE RADIO

Did you listen to the radio?
Did you hear what was on the radio?
Did you hear what was said on the radio?
Did you hear of the earth?
Did you hear of the warming of the earth?
Did you hear of the rising of the waters of the oceans of the earth?
Did you hear of the extinction of the species of the life of the earth?
Do you want to hear what I want to do with this poem of the earth?
I want to change this poem of the earth.
I want to change this poem the way I changed the station of the radio to blues not the earth's.

MY STUDENT

She was my student.
I was in love with her.
I used to say I was in love with all my pretty students.
My colleagues soon realized I wasn't.
They soon realized I would say I was only because I was a poet.
But I really was in love with her.
Her name was Victoria Harris.
She died.
When she died, she became Victoria Lauren Harris.
She is dead, but she is still my student.
She is dead, but I am still in love with her.
She is dead, but she is still Victoria Harris.
I take that back.
Victoria Harris is not dead.
She is not dead, not yet.
Victoria Harris will die on the day that I die.
And I am not dead, not yet.
Not yet.

SHIT

I was at the kitchen window.
I was looking out but seeing nothing.
It was what I wanted.
I was drinking coffee at the kitchen window.
I wanted to look out and see nothing.
Suddenly, I saw something.
I saw a brilliant red flash of red.
I saw a flame flare up.
I saw a blaze leap up from a branch tip.
I saw my old Zippo lighter.
It was the one I used to light my cigarettes.
It was the one I used to light the cigarettes of girls.
I saw a cardinal.
I saw a male cardinal in his best brilliant red.
He was sitting on the branch shitting.
I wish I had done what I wanted.
I wish I had not seen anything.
Shit, the beautiful red bird shits.
Just like Celia.

HOW TO FOLD
Inspired by a poem with the same title by Terrance Hayes

Keep the poker face on.
You may show the whisper of a smile to keep up appearances.
Put the cards face down in a perfect pile directly in front of you.
It should look like a single card five cards thick.
Do not push the pile of cards forward.
Fold your arms.
Fold your hands on the table.
Fold your arms.
Count to three to yourself.
Get up.
Go to the refrigerator.
Get a beer.
Go out on the porch or the patio or the deck or the street.
Look up at the stars.
Say, "I am lucky at love. I am lucky at love. O, yes, I am lucky at love."

DEAF CHILD AREA

I have driven the road
many times, but have
never seen the deaf child,
not in the driveway, not in
the yard, not in the window.
But the sign has been there
a long time, so the child
may no longer be around.
I'd like to think just that.
I'd like to think the deaf
child grew up, went to
college, married, moved
away to start a life. I'd like
to think the parents, now
old and alone in the house,
left the sign there to say to
us drivers passing by, "Slow
down. Open the window.
Open your ears. Hear the
birds. Hear the horses. Hear
the wind. Hear the laughter
of the years."

MINDS

Like you, Alfred, I once
had a mind different from
my mind, but it wasn't like
your mind which was "a little
butterfly/That floated away in
the silvery distance." It was a
silver mind without shape that
turned black over the years,
that tarnished because I never
polished it because I never cared
for it because I never cared for it.

ROSES

Like you, Alfred, I, too,
"thought of the rose and its thorns,"
for once I had roses, red ones
with thorns, sharp ones that never
let me forget they were roses
and not lilies, roses and not irises,
roses and not marigolds. But oh, red
roses, you fickle lovers, I forgot,
I forget, and now I miss you to death.

WHISKEY

Unlike you, Alfred, I
do not think that "Scotch is
reasonable," for I've heard
it said by an expert, a connoisseur,
an aficionado of all things whiskey,
how much "Scotch goes down
the way bourbon comes up."

TIME

Did you answer your own
question, Alfred, when you
asked, "Are you afraid of time?"
I think you did. I'm sure you
did. I think you said, "Yes,
I'm afraid of time." I'm sure
you did. I'm sure you said, "You
bet I am." I'm sure you did. I'm
sure you said, "I'm a poet, and
poets are afraid of time." I'm sure
you did. I'm sure you said, "And
poets are more afraid of time than
anyone," that is, if you answered
your own question at all, Alfred,
winding the clock in the parlor,
absorbed in its silvery key.

MOONS

"The moon is a swan in June,"
you said, Alfred, and I agree,
but you never said what it is,
the moon, in July. Why? I think
you didn't want to say that the
moon is a butterfly in July, a small
white butterfly alight on the great
black July flower of night. Too bad.
I would have agreed again.

ALL THE REST

Like you, Alfred, I, too, "never
played pool with all the rest."
I played only with my brother
and father in the pool hall on
Allerton, but I would glance over
at all the rest smoking the cigarettes,
drinking the beer, joking about the
skirts, and I wished I were of them,
one of all the rest playing pool.

LATE JULY PASTORAL

On such a day so fine as this,
how can you not feel sorry
for whatever does not fly?
How can you not feel pity
for whatever is not a tree in
the breeze beckoned to the blue?

SIX CROWS AND THEIR SHADOWS

Six crows and their shadows
crossed across as though twelve crows
crossed, but the hummingbirds at the feeder,
preoccupied as the three of them were
only with themselves, were unperturbed.

DEMENTIA

The aide was feeding
her blueberries, big blueberries,
two at a time from a tablespoon.
"You like them, don't you?" asked the aide.
She smiled and nodded.
"I like grapes," she said,
taking a blueberry from the spoon
to put in her mouth.

UNBURDENED

The tiny white flowers
are on stems so delicate they
bow under the weight
of a single fly.

WHAT'S IN A NAME

My daughter objects to a sign
on the highway that reads, *Stony Kill Farm.*
"Why would you use *kill* in the name for a farm?
Do they slaughter all the animals?" she wants to know.
"It's a Dutch word. It means stream or creek or brook," I say.
"Then they should call it *Stony Brook Farm,*" she says, "and they
ought to bring all the animals there for a bath every day."

COWARD

Had I not been, had I not been
all of that coward then,
I would have followed her there and then,
have gotten up and followed her out
onto Fifth Avenue and have followed her
north on Fifth Avenue, and oh, had I not been all
of that coward then, would have followed her north to Montreal.

READING

I don't read much anymore.
I used to read a lot. I used to
read two, three, maybe four
books at once. Non-fiction
mostly, history, biography,
popular books on science but
also novels and short stories.
I used to do that, but I don't
anymore. Poetry is just about
all I read these days and not so
much of that either. I get tired.
I get impatient. I lose interest.
I started a biography of Stephen
Crane. I got tired. I got impatient.
I lost interest. I started the biography
of Alexander Hamilton. I got tired.
I got impatient. I lost interest. I
started three novels by Samuel
Beckett. I got tired. I got impatient.
I lost interest. Jim has stopped giving
me books to read. He knows I get
tired. He knows I get impatient. He
knows I lose interest.

ST. ANNE

In my town, on the main road,
there is a church for sale, St.
Anne's Roman Catholic. Do
you think St. Anne, mother of
Mary, maternal grandmother
of Jesus, patroness of unmarried
women, housewives, women in
labor or who want to be pregnant,
grandmothers, mothers, educators,
horseback riders, cabinet makers,
and miners, knows her church is for
sale? What do you think she would
say if she knew? "And now where
will they go, all my unmarried women,
all my housewives, all my women in
labor or want to be pregnant, all my
grandmothers, all my mothers, all
my educators, all my horseback riders,
all my cabinet makers, all my miners
of my town? Where, where will they go?"

THISTLES

You three thistles, tall,
bespoke in purple, what
do you guard there by
the roadside? Sentinels,
bayonets forever fixed
and outwardly pointed,
who is it you protect? Ah,
of course, the Queen Anne's Lace.

IN THE STORE

Into the store came
a lovely mother
and her daughter
lovelier still as though
a mysterious wish
had been granted.

PHYSICAL THERAPY

Because he looked like her father,
because he looked like her father many years gone,
her eyes lit up with memory,
and she smiled and kept smiling and
continued to smile until
he who was her father long gone was gone,
until the smile she smiled for her father long gone was gone,
gone back to where it had come from.

ORTHODOX PARADOX

After so much rain,
the sun was heaven-sent,
but so was the rain.

SHORT AUGUST PASTORAL

The breeze plays rough.
It becomes wind.

The petunias laugh in its face.
Why not? They survived the storms of July.

The wind chimes mark time in the wind it becomes.
But they do not chime.

The Virginia creeper puts its arm around the fence's shoulder.
It is the fence's best friend.

The hummingbird feeder fills with ants.
Filled with sugar, they die a happy death.

My three hummingbirds do not care.
They see the shadows have moved from here to there.

MARGIE

I asked my friend, Rob, why he
named his motorcycle *Margie*.
He laughed and told me about
the time he went on a road trip
and stopped in a small town in
Vermont. He doesn't remember
the name, but it was near Rutland.
Anyway, it had a bar, so he went
in for a beer or two. The barmaid
had tattoos, a nose ring, long dark
hair and was beautiful. She told
him her name was "Margie" and
winked at him. He smiled at her,
gave her a big tip, and decided to
stay the night at the hotel next to
the bar. As he was registering, the
clerk asked him if he had been to
the bar. They have good beer he
said, but if he does go in, he should
"watch out for Margie." He thanked
the clerk, went up to his room, fell
asleep, checked out at six, got on his
Triumph, revved it up, and said,
"Let's go! Watch out for Margie!"

PART II

I, TOO, HAVE NOWHERE

to go, Ammons,
so why not go together
since, at least today,
we're going each other's way?

I, TOO, HAVE BEEN MARRIED

a long time, Ammons,
longer than you when
you confessed your
faithfulness with such wit,
but not for lack of trying.
It's been the tack of lying, I think.

I, TOO, LEARN FROM THE LAKE

I, too, learn from the lake,
Ammons, for like yours,
mine teaches by example
the one lesson all lakes
learn soon or late.

THE BIG HORNETS

The big hornets
at the feeder have driven
the hummingbird away

and back into the trees
where it waits to come back
to the sugar water prepared for it.

SYMPATHY

One white butterfly
is enough for here
for now,

but the other
for which
it searches

in vain,
I, too, search
in vain for.

SQUATTERS IN THE PLANTER

Squatters in the planter
in which
no flowers were planted,

the wild grasses
have taken it.
"It is ours now,"

they proclaim.
"See how we
improve this barren

property you neglected.
You can remove
us by force

if you choose,
but you will sleep
badly if you do."

MY PLUMBER IS A SCULPTOR

My plumber is a sculptor.
He's exhibited in the library
and the gallery of the local
college. His mailbox is
a locomotive, correct in
every detail, the cow catcher
facing the road. It's the only
place where I see the driver
of the postal truck smile.

AUGUST LAMENT

Hard to believe that
the peonies, shriveled,
shrunken, now burnt black
down to nothing more than
match heads, were once
gorgeous, the garden's
glory, and harder still that
the ornamental cherry was
once exactly that, April's
ornament, and hardest of all,
that once it was – Was what? –
April at all.

NINA SIMONE

My neighbor, Harry, is 90.
He needs hearing aids.
He says when two people
are talking, he can hear only
the person with the higher
voice. He says he can't hear
the person with the low voice,
especially if it's a woman
with a low voice. That means
he's missing the smokey, sultry
voices of the likes of Lauren
Bacall and Kathleen Turner and
Nina Simone. Oh, of Nina Simone.

BALCONY

The hotel room had a balcony.
From the balcony, I could see across
the road, busy with traffic day and night,
and beyond the road, another hotel
with balconies facing the road and my hotel.
This is not what a balcony is for.
A balcony is for seeing a river or a waterfall.
A balcony is for watching a horse disappear across a field.

BEYOND THE PALE

What have they done?
What have they built if not
a new ghetto, risen,
and continuing to rise, on
the town's highest hill?
No need for walls, though,
for each housing unit is tall
as any wall. Look, already
there's a plastic tricycle,
there's an old mattress,
there's a broken clay pot
with dead flowers, all in
the ditch by the highway.

MOMENTOUS

A moment of silence
between the engines
and motors, of quiet
amid kids' cacophonies,
of a brazen blast of peace,
of a bearhug of blessing,
is momentous this afternoon,
short and to the point.

DEBATE

One said the sun is conscious,
and to prove it, he proposed
an experiment in which a million
Hindus in India would ask the sun
to emit three quick solar flares at
a specified time, noon on Sunday,
say, which if it did, would certainly
demonstrate that the sun is indeed
conscious. The other rolled her eyes,
then stared at him, quickly, three times.

NO CONTEST

If given the choice,
I'd prefer a pony's
clip-clop
to a phony's
hip-hop.

DEMENTIA

Her friend of forty years called.
Her friend said, "Hello. Can you hear me?"
She took the phone from the caregiver's hand.
She said, "Hi."
Her friend said, "Are you listening to music?"
She said, "Yes."
Then her friend said something.
Then she fell silent.
Then the phone fell from her hand.
Then the darkness fell over face once more.
Then her head fell over to one side.
Then her friend of forty years said, "I'll visit soon,"
    into the darkness.
Then her friend of forty years fell silent.

IN THE LIQUOR STORE

I went to the liquor store to buy
a bottle of Italian red wine. As I
was leaving, I spotted an Irish
whiskey called *Writers' Tears.*
The owner happened to be standing
there, so I told him that if it were
called *Poets' Tears,* I'd buy it,
even though it cost $43. Why? he
said. I'm a poet, I said. I know you
are. I have a couple of your books.
But you do write the poems, don't
you? he said. Sure, I write down
the poems, but I'm not a writer. I'm
a poet, I said. Aren't poets writers?
he said. No. We poets don't consider
ourselves writers. We're the poets.
The writers are all the other guys.
The guys who write novels. The guys
who write short stories. The guys
who write non-fiction books. The guys
who write magazine articles, I said.
I get it. Poet doesn't rhyme with writer,
he said. I paused a second. You know,
that's a good way to put it, I said, leaving
with my bottle of Montepulciano d'Abruzzo.

THE JOURNEY

I stand under the wild black cherry.
It is September.
The leaves are starting to turn.
They are turning slowly, a few at a time.
They are starting to fall.
I stand under the wild black cherry now
the way I stood under it five months ago.
It was April, and the white cherry blossoms
were falling. The petals fell then as the leaves
now fall. "Thank you, Old Man Cherry,
for reminding me of our journey together," I say.
"I will meet you in the spring when
your white beard is full of bees once again."

SOUL

When I dead-head
the dead marigolds,
when I snap the brown
ones, the dry ones, off
the stems, I inhale the living
fragrance the dead flowers
leave on my fingers so deeply,
so much more deeply than other breath,
that I want to stand there next to the headless stems
and breathe in that fragrance on my fingers
until I have all, every last molecule of marigold
deep inside, deep in the place where it's said there's a soul.

THE FACE

Today I beheld a face that was the face
that if 1,000 ships could be launched by a face
would be that one face and no other face,
a young woman's face,
surely no more than a girl's face,
a server in a restaurant on the waterfront's face,
surely it should be named *Troy* (for her face)
but alas, why a nose ring-ruined face,
to which I wanted to say, "Not in this face,
no nose ring to ruin this face
that if 1,000 ships could be launched by a face
would be this one face and no other face."
O, how dare I say that to her face?
Ah, now I dare say anything, anything, to the world's face.

LIKE YOU, ALFRED

Like you, Alfred, I, too,
"wanted to know more about
the cardinal," so I stood up
and followed him (Yes, he
was, for he was as red as a
fire engine!) as far as I could,
which was the tree he stopped
in for a while before disappearing,
appearing unfollowable.

UNLIKE YOU, ALFRED

Unlike you, Alfred, I did not
"wonder if we weren't lonely
for the golden dark smiles" as
I, at least, had no need to wonder,
for I knew, knew down below
all known things, I was lonely for
them, those smiles, not dark golden
but golden dark, yes, as you knew.

A HAWK WITH A BROKEN WING   IS A HAWK BROKEN

A hawk with a broken wing is a hawk broken.
A broken bird.

It gives up the sky for a perch perpetual.
It forgets feathers but remembers what talons are for.

A branch chewed half through by claws is its prey.
A broken hawk hops from low to lower.

A broken hawk jumps from lower to low.
A broken hawk has a broken eye also.

It has a short sky that does not require a hawk's unbroken eye.
A canopy with no view of the sky is their kindest kindness.

COLUMBUS

Columbus changed his mind.
The world is not round,

after all, he said in his diary,
It is not a ball,

not a globe.
No, the world is shaped

like a pear, he said in his diary.
It is a woman's breast,

and this mountain
on this east coast of India

is the highest point,
the nipple atop

the breast of the world,
and these waters

spilling down from it,
its milk, he said in his diary,

licking his lips.

FALSE MESSIAH

We have stopped
the full-page ads
in the newspaper
and taken his picture

down from the signs
in Brooklyn.
We have cancelled
the charters to the Holy Land.

We have shorn our side-locks
and rent our cassocks.
We have sanctified our kitchens
and shut in our women.

We have ordered new ink,
new paper, new books.
We have told the carpenters
to measure oak for new chairs.

We have screwed new bulbs tight
into the sockets of our lights.
We have begged our children
for their forgiveness. Amen.

A PHOTOGRAPH OF WILLIAM CARLOS WILLIAMS

He is laughing,
perhaps at what someone is saying,
but more likely at what he is saying.
His face is laughing,
his whole face is laughing,
his mouth, his eyes behind his glasses,
his eyebrows above his glasses duplicating
the curve of his glasses,
his chin, all are laughing.
His necktie is laughing
tucked under his collar which
is laughing around his neck which
is laughing.
His necktie is laughing at both ends.
His shirt is laughing
out from behind his necktie
and the two shirt pockets, one
buttoned and one unbuttoned are laughing,
but the unbuttoned pocket is laughing the louder.
His jacket is laughing,
a big belly laugh all around him.
His hands are laughing,
one hand laughing in his pants' pocket,
the other hand laughing on his waist, holding
his belt which is smiling and in a moment will laugh.

RHINOCEROS HEAD

He looks as though he hasn't slept
in weeks, the brown glass eyes softly sad,
the skin beneath folded and sagged.

He wasn't meant to be seen
from such an unnatural angle,
we down here gazing at him

up there above us on the wall.
We want to reach up and rub his chin.
We want to toss a hat onto his horn.

Sweetness, all sweetness he is,
like a great, wrinkled gray rose,
with a shark's fin for a thorn.

THE BEST NAMES IN POETRY

Russell Banks
      Coleman Barks
            Ellen Bass

Marvin Bell
      Wendell Berry
            Elizabeth Bishop

David Bottoms
      Robert Bridges
            Gwendolyn Brooks

Basil Bunting
      Robert Burns
            Kelly Cherry

Wendy Cope
      Hart Crane
            Stephen Crane

Rita Dove
> Edward Field
>> Carol Frost

Robert Frost
> Oliver Goldsmith
>> Robert Graves

Thomas Gray
> Barbara Guest
>> Edgar Guest

Donald Hall
> Thomas Hood
>> Donald Justice

Alicia Keys
> Etheridge Knight
>> Thomas Lux

David Mason
> Edgar Lee Masters
>> Howard Moss

Thylias Moss

    Octavio Paz

        Molly Peacock

Thomas Love Peacock

    Alexander Pope

        Ezra Pound

John Crowe Ransom

    David Ray

        Henry Reed

Ishmael Reed

    Adrienne Rich

        Robert Service

Anne Sexton

    Tom Sleigh

        Christopher Smart

Cathy Song

    Gerald Stern

        Ruth Stone

Mark Strand
      Jonathan Swift
            Madeline Tiger

Jean Valentine
      Robert Penn Warren
            Yvor Winters

WHEN THE BUDDHA WAS 80 YEARS OLD

When the Buddha was 80 years old
and about to die, he said
to his followers,
Make of yourself a light.
It is not recorded
that one leaned over
and whispered in his ear,
Enlightened One, tell us,
is it not also good
to make of yourself
the reflection of a light?
The Buddha's answer
was likewise not passed down.
It was: *Yes, that is also good.*

A GREEN GLASS BOTTLE

A green glass bottle, unopened, and a red
aluminum can, also unopened, exposed,
strangely side by side as though embracing,
in the weeds of the ditch at the side of the road
newly mown by the town mower, this virgin
couple buried in one grave, this peace sacrifice
of these feuding tribes of trash.

ANGINA

It is a hand on the heart,
a greeting.
It is mortality grinning,
dumbly, with its big,

hearty hand on the heart,
mortality in person,
squeezing the heart
with its big, hot hand.

And then it becomes
remembering,
the heart remembering
painful experiences

from its infancy,
its childhood and its youth,
separations in the dark,
nightmares of falling

and chases through forests,
unrequited love for heroines
of books and movie stars,
an ache in the shape

of a hand holding such
a heavy heart heart-level
and too long to bear.
It is Latin for *torture*.

WHERE

I saw it today, where
I want to be buried.
It's the cemetery next
to the apple orchard.
It doesn't have to be
this cemetery and this
orchard, as long as it's
a cemetery next to an
orchard, and as long as
I'm as close to the apple
trees as the local laws
allow, and if possible, closer.

About the Author

Nominated for the National Book Award, the Eric Hoffer Book Award, and nominated three times for the Pulitzer Prize, J.R. Solonche is the author of 40 books of poetry and coauthor of another. He lives in the Hudson Valley.

Author photograph by Emily Solonche

Other books by J. R. Solonche
published by Dos Madres Press

True Enough (2019)
To Say The Least (2019)
In A Public Place (2019)
Dust (2021)
The Lost Notebook of Zhao Li (2022)
Leda (2023)

For the full Dos Madres Press catalog:
www.dosmadres.com